Contents

Nature's tricks

Imagine seeing fish raining from the sky or lightning that chases people. Tingles run up your spine. You shake your head, blink your eyes and become suspicious. How can this be happening? Perhaps it's just a trick. You want to **investigate**, but your heart pounds and your palms sweat. It might not be safe. If the rules of nature are being broken, what else may go wrong?

You wouldn't be the only one asking these questions. Some of the greatest minds in the world have puzzled over these same mysteries. They look for clues to get answers. They propose **explanations**. Get ready to explore some of nature's most puzzling mysteries!

investigate gather facts in order to discover as much as possible about an event or person

explanation statement made to clarify something and make it understandable

4

Falling fish

All over the world, fish have rained from the sky. When fish drop from the clouds, people can't believe their eyes. They call out to their friends to make sure they aren't seeing things. Then they start to worry. What else may rain down on their heads?

People question whether this event really happens. It seems like a **hoax**. But many times throughout history, people have reported bizarre things falling from the sky. The falling items are often fish, but not always. Many of these strange happenings have occurred in the UK. Minnows rained down on people in Knighton, Wales, in 2004. In Coventry, a storm of apples brought traffic to a halt in 2011. In London, hundreds of dead frogs rained down in 1998.

hoax trick to make people believe something that is not true

Some items reported falling from the sky

Item	Location	Date
alligators	South Carolina, USA	1877
jellyfish	Frankston, Australia	1935
maggots	Acapulco, Mexico	1967
frogs	London, England	1998
minnows	Knighton, Wales	2004
apples	Coventry, England	2011

Are storms to blame?

Scientists say strong winds from nearby storms may be to blame. The fish in Knighton were found just after a thunderstorm. The apples in Coventry fell on a day when storms were predicted. The frogs in London fell during a shower of rain. **Waterspouts**, which may develop when storms pass over water, can whip wind at over 160 kilometres (100 miles) per hour. Is that enough power to suck things up into the sky?

Something fishy

People wonder about this answer. Firstly, it has not been proven that waterspouts are strong enough to pick up thousands of items. Secondly, the items are usually all the same thing. How could the wind choose what it picks up?

Will this mystery ever be solved? It is difficult to predict when and where the next bizarre shower of objects will happen. Without this information it is hard to collect **evidence**. And without solid evidence, it may remain a mystery for a long time.

waterspout mass of spinning cloud-filled wind that stretches from a cloud to a body of water

evidence information, items and facts that help prove something is true or false

Death Valley's sliding stones

In Death Valley in California, USA, large stones sit at the end of long winding grooves in the desert sand. It is obvious that the stones have slid into place, but can this be possible? There are no footprints. There are no tyre tracks. There are no signs that point to people. It is as though a ghost slid each stone across the desert.

Clues

Some say the wind is to blame. Is it strong enough? It might need some assistance. Let's examine the evidence. Firstly, the rocks travelled in the same direction as the wind. The desert wind howls up to 145 kilometres (90 miles) per hour in this environment. Secondly, it rains in this desert a few times a year. Although the temperature is usually scorching hot, occasionally it dips below freezing. A slippery surface caused by wind gusts and freezing rain may be the **culprit**.

Another culprit may be a **bacterium** that lives in the desert sand. When it rains, the bacterium becomes wet and gets slimy. Perhaps it makes the sand slippery. Then the rocks could glide along the ground when the wind blows.

Recent discovery

Using high-power cameras and tracking devices, scientists caught the rocks in motion in 2014. During rare instances of below-freezing temperatures, thin sheets of ice were blown by the wind and rammed into the rocks. Bit by bit the ice shoved the rocks downwind. Scientists will continue to collect evidence until they are sure that they have the answer.

culprit cause of a problem or defect

bacterium single-celled microscopic creature that exists everywhere in nature

Disappearing bees

A swarming, buzzing beehive suddenly goes silent. The honeycomb, eggs and newborn bees sit eerily still. The adult bees have vanished. Why would the bees leave their home? In the winter of 2005–2006, thousands and thousands of adult honeybees in the United States disappeared from their hives without a trace. There were no dead bees, no clues as to where the bees went and no evidence that explained why they left. Not long after, reports of bee disappearances came pouring in from across North America and Europe.

Worse still, bees continue to disappear. People are beginning to wonder if all of the bees will vanish. Many experts agree that there must be more than one cause for the vanishing bees. That makes it extra tricky to solve this mystery.

Give a bee a helping hand

Do you enjoy crunchy almonds or sweet cherries? Without bees these foods would not exist. Bees **pollinate** these plants. Disappearing bees is a very serious problem, but you can make a difference:

- Plant bee-friendly flowers in your garden.
- Teach your family about bees' role in the environment.

pollinate transfer pollen from plant to plant; pollination helps flowers make seeds

The suspects

In the summer of 2012, a scientist at Harvard University in Massachusetts, USA, fed bees in 12 different hives a certain **pesticide**. Later that winter, the bees abandoned their hives. Bees that were not fed the pesticide stayed in their homes. More hives need to be studied before conclusions can be made.

A **parasite** could also be at fault. Tiny parasites, such as Varroa mites, drink the blood of bees and spread viruses throughout colonies. But no one has proven that the parasites cause bee colonies to mysteriously vanish.

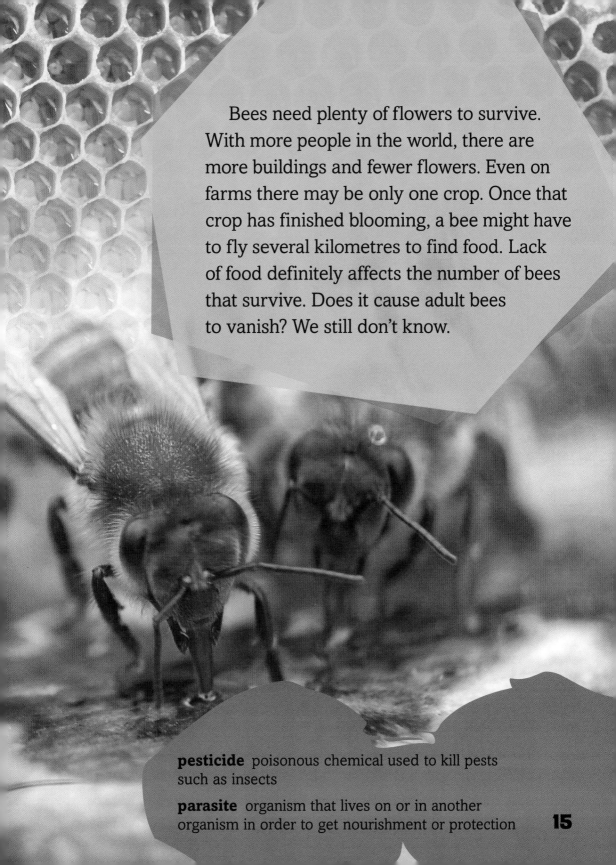

Bees need plenty of flowers to survive. With more people in the world, there are more buildings and fewer flowers. Even on farms there may be only one crop. Once that crop has finished blooming, a bee might have to fly several kilometres to find food. Lack of food definitely affects the number of bees that survive. Does it cause adult bees to vanish? We still don't know.

pesticide poisonous chemical used to kill pests such as insects

parasite organism that lives on or in another organism in order to get nourishment or protection

Monsters from the sea

A long-horned beast, a hairless creature, gooey grey blobs – dead animals creep up on beaches around the world. What are these mystery monsters?

When an unknown animal washes up on shore, people get excited. Everyone has a guess. Perhaps it's a new creature we have never seen before. Or it could be an animal rarely seen by people, such as a giant squid. It can be fun to guess what types of animal these are and where they came from, but it's still puzzling how they got onto the beaches.

Case closed?

Sometimes these mysteries turn out to be pretty easy to solve. When a snake-like body washed up on a beach in Scotland in 2011, people called it a monster. But a vet imagined the missing parts. He knew it was just part of a baby whale. Slimy grey globs found in Chile in 2003? Only blubber – nothing that exciting.

A mysterious blob washed up on a beach in the United States in 2005. The blob was actually a giant squid.

Other instances of washed-up animals remain a mystery. In 2008 a four-legged body came ashore in New York, USA. Some say it was a raccoon, others claim it was a dog and still others say it was a fake object created to cause confusion. To this day the object remains a mystery to many. Each new dead creature that washes up is a mystery to be solved.

Africa's barren polka dots

A dry grassland in Namibia, Africa, is dotted with bare orange circles. In a landscape usually covered in grass, these dead zones do not make sense. They are like a rash on the earth. Will they spread across the world? What causes the mysterious circles? Scientists from around the world have travelled to south-west Africa to try to clear up these unanswered questions.

The details

The circles are 2.1 to 12 metres (7 to 39 feet) across. No plants grow inside the circles. Just outside of the circles, however, grasses often grow three times taller than other grasses in the area. Do the barren circles have special growing powers?

Namibia's barren circles dot the landscape and remain a mystery.

Good guesses

People claim that dragons, gods or UFOs made the circles. Some say the circles are hoaxes. Scientists have other **hypotheses**.

Scientists wonder if a barren circle is the result of an underground war for water. They know that circles are most common where there is little rain. They found that the soil near the edge of a circle is even drier than in the centre. These researchers propose that the grass on the edge sucks the circle dry.

One scientist found sand termites in every circle. Perhaps the termites eat the grass. However, others question that idea. How could the termites cause the spots to be in a circular shape?

Not many people want to spend money to study soil and grass. So it may be a while before this mystery gets solved.

hypothesis prediction that can be tested about how a scientific investigation or experiment will turn out

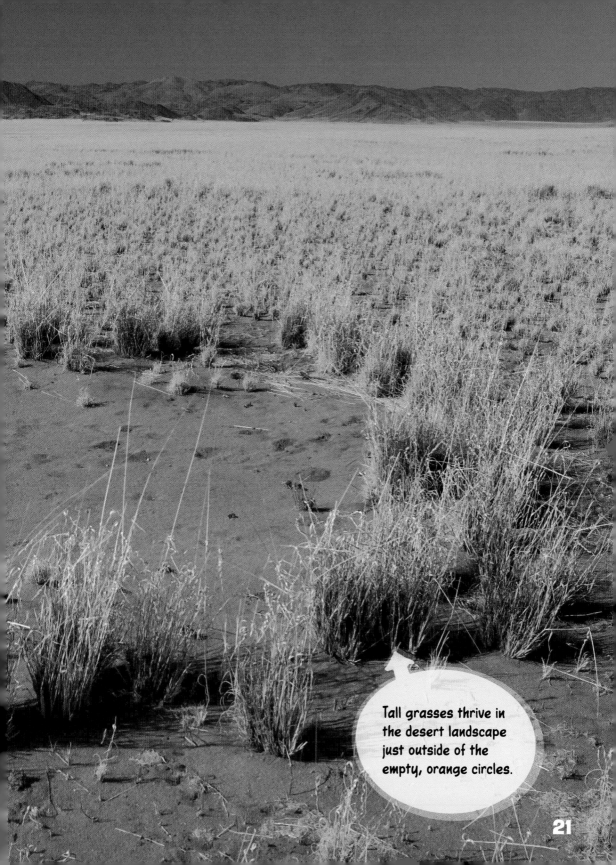

Tall grasses thrive in the desert landscape just outside of the empty, orange circles.

Freaky frogs

In August 1995, a group of schoolchildren pulled deformed frogs out of Ney Pond in the northern United States. There weren't just one or two strange frogs. More than half of the frogs had missing legs, missing eyes or extra hind legs.

After a newspaper story about the frogs was released, more reports came tumbling in. Odd frogs were popping up all over North America – in parts of Minnesota, Ohio, Texas and in Ontario, Canada. What was going on?

The problems

This mystery isn't simple to study. After the **deformities** were discovered, the frogs in Ney Pond vanished for the winter. Pupils found them under the ice in a nearby river. Because the frogs travelled during their life cycle, scientists had to search for evidence in the pond, on land and in the river. There were many things, such as pollution in their environment, that could have affected the frogs. It was impossible to study every one of them.

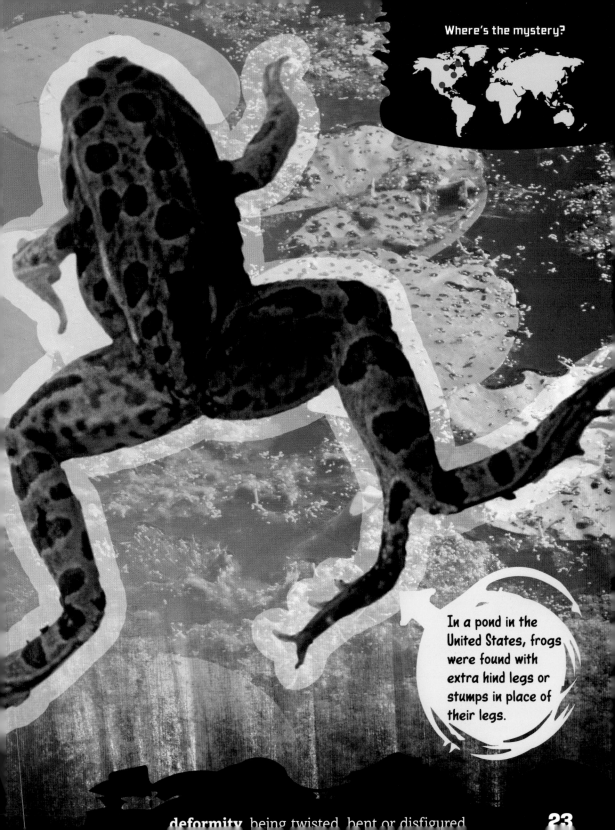

In a pond in the United States, frogs were found with extra hind legs or stumps in place of their legs.

deformity being twisted, bent or disfigured

What's to blame?

After 20 years, scientists still have no explanation. Why? It's not a straightforward case. Pollution might be the cause. Frogs can take in water and air through their skin. That means they also soak up chemicals from the water. In a laboratory, when scientists grew tadpoles in polluted water, the tadpoles were damaged. Did chemicals in Ney Pond cause the deformities?

Other experts believe that a parasite living inside the tadpoles caused the frogs' legs to grow incorrectly. Laboratory tests were conducted. The deformities caused by that parasite did not match the deformities found in frogs living in Ney Pond.

It is possible that more than one factor caused the frog deformities. But we still don't have an answer.

This American bullfrog was discovered with six legs. Scientists aren't sure what caused the deformity.

Balls of lightning

A ball of lightning floats above the ground. It zigs, it zags and then it heads straight towards you. It disappears. Ball lightning is bizarre. Normal lightning doesn't float across the ground. It doesn't seem intelligent. And it doesn't chase people. Ball lightning does. Once, it even bounced on a teacher's head – 20 times! What's even more bizarre is that no one knows exactly what it is or what's in it.

What we think we know

Ball lightning can be as small as a marble or as big as a car. Often it is the size of an orange. Ball lightning is usually red, but it also can be white, blue, purple or green. Ball lightning can bounce, climb or blast through a wall. Often it floats silently.

Because the balls seem to know where they are going, some people claim they are intelligent and possibly are aliens from another galaxy. Others think they are mini **black holes** or explosions from secret military tests.

black hole area in space around a collapsed star whose gravity sucks in everything around it, even light

Sprites, Jets and Elves

From high above the clouds, astronauts have had great views of other spooky forms of lightning. Scientists classify odd lightning into different types:

Red Sprites: red or green flashes that are shaped like jellyfish and seen high above storm clouds

Blue Jets: bright blue cones of light, stretching about 40 kilometres (25 miles) up from the top of a cloud

Elves: flat, glowing lights that last just a millisecond but swell up to 320 kilometres (200 miles) across

People spotted an incredible ball of lightning in the Netherlands in 2011.

Making lightning

Scientists have tried to reconstruct models of lightning to help answer their questions. With salt water, electricity and a clay tube, experts in Berlin, Germany, created a floating, glowing ball of **plasma**. Did they create ball lightning?

Plasma clouds, which are similar to ball lightning, were created in a laboratory in Germany in 2006.

One researcher thinks ball lightning is made of **silica**. He proposed that normal lightning hits the ground and **vaporizes** silica. The chemical then rises as a ball and burns. But other scientists say this can't be the full story. They have watched lightning hit the ground hundreds of times and have never seen ball lightning.

Any answers?

If the experts can't agree, will we ever know what ball lightning is? Some of the brightest minds in the world are still desperate to find answers.

Still searching

The mysteries of nature are like puzzles. Finding solutions requires careful searching, seeking out hidden evidence and proving an explanation. For many of these mysteries, people have found clues and made hypotheses. Yet experts are still looking for solid answers.

Why do fish fall from the sky? What strange creatures are crawling out of the sea? Can ball lightning really chase a person? Perhaps one day you could be involved in solving one of these strange mysteries!

plasma highly charged state of matter that is usually formed only inside stars

silica chemical found in sand

vaporize convert into vapour or fine particles of mist, steam or smoke that can be seen hanging in the air

Glossary

bacterium single-celled microscopic creature that exists everywhere in nature

black hole area in space around a collapsed star whose gravity sucks in everything around it, even light

culprit cause of a problem or defect

deformity being twisted, bent or disfigured

evidence information, items and facts that help prove something is true or false

explanation statement made to clarify something and make it understandable

hoax trick to make people believe something that is not true

hypothesis prediction that can be tested about how a scientific investigation or experiment will turn out

investigate gather facts in order to discover as much as possible about an event or person

parasite organism that lives on or in another organism in order to get nourishment or protection

pesticide poisonous chemical used to kill pests such as insects

plasma highly charged state of matter that is usually formed only inside stars

pollinate transfer pollen from plant to plant; pollination helps flowers make seeds

silica chemical found in sand

waterspout mass of spinning cloud-filled wind that stretches from a cloud to a body of water

vaporize convert into vapour or fine particles of mist, steam or smoke that can be seen hanging in the air

Books

Crop Circles (Solving Mysteries with Science), Jane Bingham (Raintree, 2013)

Plants (The Science Behind…), Rachel Lynette (Raintree, 2012)

Usborne Illustrated Book of Nature, Phillip Clarke (Usborne Publishing Ltd, 2009)

Websites

www.bbc.co.uk/nature
Discover interesting facts, photos and videos about nature.

www.naturedetectives.org.uk
Learn more about nature and the seasons.

www.ngkids.co.uk/did-you-know/Honey-Bees
Find fascinating facts about honeybees!

Index